# EXPLORATION AND ENCOUNTERS

# Contents

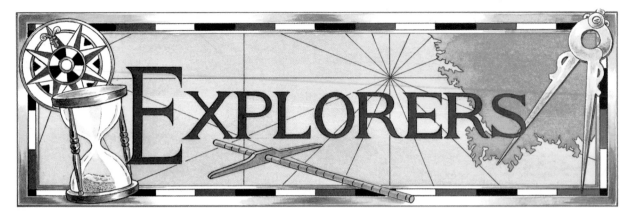

# EXPLORERS

Today we know exactly what our world looks like. <u>Satellites</u> can take pictures of the earth from space. We can draw maps to show the shape of each country. Travellers can fly to other countries and take photographs of the people and animals that live there.

In 1450, most people did not travel far from the place where they were born.

They did not go on holidays to other countries. Travelling was much harder than it is today. There were no aeroplanes, trains or cars.

Foreign lands were a mystery. Those explorers who did sail to other countries did not have cameras to take with them. They returned with stories of strange people and fantastic animals.

## Why did people want to explore?

# LOOKING AT EVIDENCE

These are some of the ways people in 1450 found out about the world.

▶ Explorers wrote about the lands and people they had seen.

*The Indians of Brazil eat the flesh of their enemies. They cut a man up in pieces which they put to dry in smoke. Every day they cut off a small piece and eat it with their ordinary food to remember their enemies.*

▼ Explorers drew maps of the countries they had travelled across. The invention of printing in 1492 meant that copies of these maps could be made for other explorers. But the maps were often wrong.

▲ Explorers brought back objects from their travels, like this mask. It was made by people called Aztecs who lived in the country we now call Mexico.

▶ Explorers drew pictures of the things they saw. This is a drawing of strange people an explorer claimed to have seen in Asia. As you can see, these drawings were often not true!

# Silks and spices

People have always wanted to buy special things from foreign countries. In the 15th century <u>silk</u> thread could only be found in the Far East, in China and Japan. Rich people in Europe wanted to buy silk to make into fine clothes. Merchants travelled on long journeys to the Far East to buy silk which they sold at a high price when they returned home.

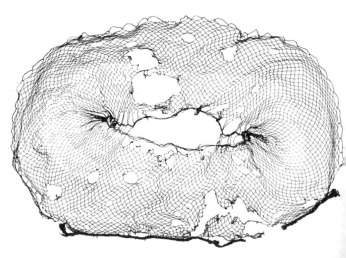

▲ This hairnet was worn in London in the 14th century. It is made from Chinese silk thread.

◄ Cooks could buy spices and grind them to powder with a pestle and mortar. Spices were used for seasoning. It was also believed that pepper could be used against poison, cinnamon for stomach-ache, and nutmeg for freckles!

Merchants also travelled to the Far East to buy spices. Spices were important in the 15th century. There were no freezers or refrigerators to keep food fresh. Foods like fish and meat were often covered in salt and dried. Cooks used spices to make dull food taste better, and to hide the taste of food that was slightly bad.

Sugar was also called a spice. Cooks needed sugar to make sweet dishes. White and brown sugar was sold in loaves which were treacly in the middle.

## Trade routes from the East

Merchants travelled overland to China and India to buy the silks and spices. These were carried back to Europe on camels and horses. But in the 1400s Turks and Tartars seized the lands of the East Mediterranean and refused to let merchants cross their land. The rulers and merchants of Europe wanted explorers to find a new way to the Far East by sea.

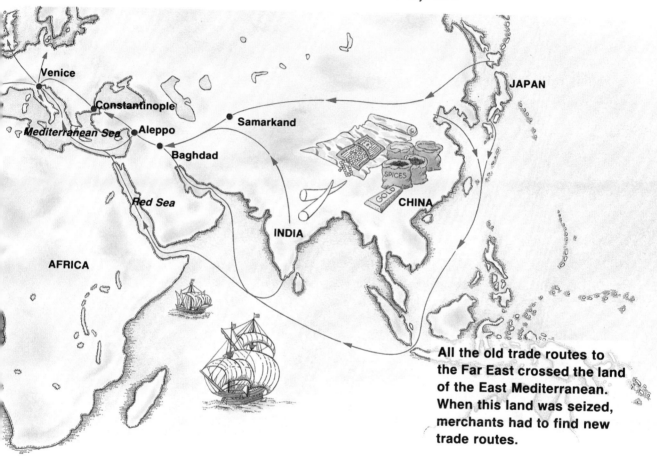

**All the old trade routes to the Far East crossed the land of the East Mediterranean. When this land was seized, merchants had to find new trade routes.**

## The Age of Exploration begins

The rulers of Spain and Portugal paid explorers to find a new way to the Far East. Many explorers sailed off into the unknown, without accurate maps to guide them or weather forecasts to warn them of storms. The years between 1450 and 1550 have since become known as the 'Age of Exploration'.

Before 1450, explorers travelled mostly overland. An explorer called Marco Polo went from Venice all the way to China (which was then called Cathay). He wrote a book about all that he had seen, but many people did not believe him. Arab travellers explored the lands between Spain and China.

Much of the world, including the great continents of America and Australia, was still unknown to Europeans (see the map on page 17).

5

# Discovering the world

**The search for new trade routes**

When the overland trading routes closed, Spanish and Portuguese explorers went to sea to find a new way to the Far East. These explorers were deadly rivals.

In 1497, Vasco da Gama of Portugal found a way to India by sailing round Africa. But the Portuguese would not let Spanish merchants sail with them.

Spanish explorers had to find their own route to the Far East. They thought that if they sailed west from Spain they would reach China. They did not realize that a great continent lay between Spain and China. The Spanish explorer Columbus sailed west to find out if this was possible, but he made an even greater discovery. In 1492 he arrived at what became known as the 'New World', which we now call North and South America. (You can find out more about Columbus on page 14.)

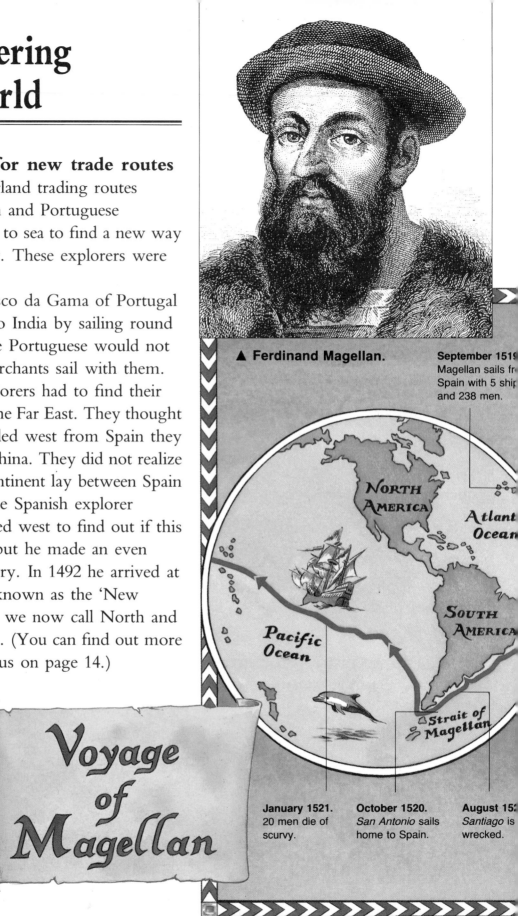

▲ Ferdinand Magellan.

**September 1519** Magellan sails from Spain with 5 ships and 238 men.

NORTH AMERICA

Atlantic Ocean

Pacific Ocean

SOUTH AMERICA

Strait of Magellan

**January 1521.** 20 men die of scurvy.

**October 1520.** *San Antonio* sails home to Spain.

**August 152** *Santiago* is wrecked.

**Voyage of Magellan**

## The voyage of Magellan

Ferdinand Magellan was born in Portugal in 1480. He had always wanted to become an explorer and had read books about the voyages of Columbus. Magellan wanted to find out if it was possible to reach the Far East by sailing west, around South America. If he could do this, he would become the first man to sail right around the world.

In 1519 the King of Spain agreed to give Magellan five ships to find this new trade route. The men in Magellan's crew came from many different countries. Magellan had to make them work together and not give up when things were bad. The captains of four of his ships were Spanish. They did not like being told what to do by a Portuguese. During the voyage three of them even tried to kill him.

The journey was long and dangerous. The ships took three months to cross the vast Pacific Ocean, without finding any land or fresh water on the way. Many of the crew died of starvation and disease.

Only one ship, the *Victoria*, arrived safely home in 1522. Of the 238 men who set out, only 18 returned. Magellan himself had been killed on the voyage. But his great journey showed that it was possible to sail right around the world.

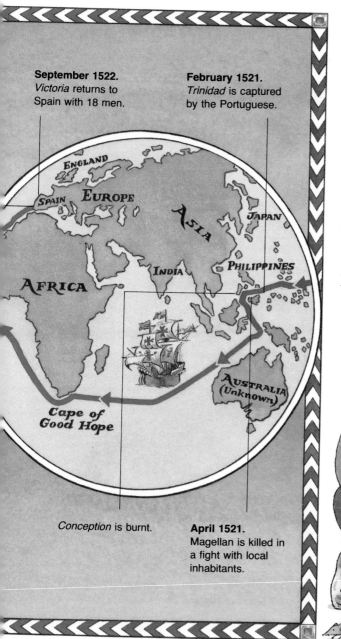

**September 1522.**
*Victoria* returns to Spain with 18 men.

**February 1521.**
*Trinidad* is captured by the Portuguese.

ENGLAND

SPAIN   EUROPE

ASIA

JAPAN

AFRICA

INDIA   PHILIPPINES

AUSTRALIA (Unknown)

Cape of
Good Hope

*Conception* is burnt.

**April 1521.**
Magellan is killed in a fight with local inhabitants.

We ate old biscuits full of grubs and drank water that was yellow and stinking. We ate rats and sawdust.

# Setting sail

Before explorers set out to sea their ships were loaded with everything they would need on their journey. Live animals were taken on board and kept in pens to be killed and eaten later. Huge amounts of food were taken. Magellan's fleet took 15 tons of biscuits and over 1,500 pounds of honey. They also took goods that could be traded for spices, like 20,000 little metal bells.

**Magellan's flagship _Trinidad_ may have looked like this.**

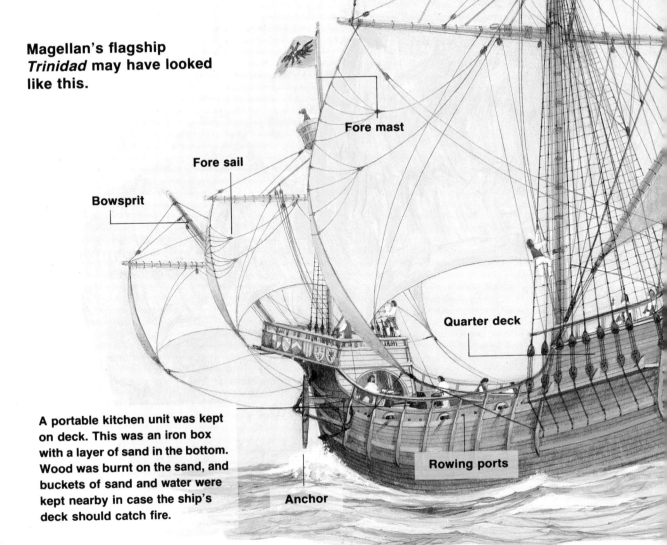

Main sail

Main mast

A sailor stood in the lookout to see ahead.

Mizzen mast

Fore mast

Fore sail

Bowsprit

Quarter deck

**A portable kitchen unit was kept on deck. This was an iron box with a layer of sand in the bottom. Wood was burnt on the sand, and buckets of sand and water were kept nearby in case the ship's deck should catch fire.**

Rowing ports

Anchor

8

## An explorer's ship

Explorers of the 15th and 16th centuries did not have steel ships with engines as we do today. Their ships were made of wooden planks fastened together with wooden pegs and iron nails. Big cloth sails were fixed to tall masts.

**Lantern**

**Poop deck**

**The leadsman stood in the sounding barrel, and lowered a piece of lead attached to a line, to find out how deep the sea was.**

**Rudder**

### Stores and cargo for Magellan's Fleet

**FOOD**

Cows, pigs and hens
Food for the animals
Dried pork and salted meat
Dried peas, beans and lentils
Garlic and onions
Rice and flour
Barrels of ship's biscuits
Cheeses
Raisins, currants and almonds
Honey, vinegar and olive oil
Salt and mustard
Casks of water and wine

**EQUIPMENT**

Wooden bowls and plates
Firewood
Iron cooking pots
Scales and balances with weights
Fishnets, fish-hooks, fish-spears
Wooden buckets
Candles, lanterns
Horns, bugles and tambourines
Seamen's chests
Ladders
Flags
Small boats and oars
Leg-irons for prisoners

**THINGS FOR REPAIRING THE SHIP**

Ropes
Spare sails and masts
Spare barrels and casks
Timber
Iron cauldron for melting pitch
Blacksmith's tools
Grindstone

**WEAPONS**

Large and small canons
Gunpowder and canon balls
Handguns
Crossbows and bolts
Javelins, pikes and lances
Armour and shields

**GOODS TO TRADE FOR SPICES**

Coloured cloth
Cloth dye
Combs
Cheap knives
Fish-hooks
Red caps and handkerchiefs
Little bells
Metals and crystals

# Life at sea

Everyone on board ship had his own work to do.

*The captain* worked out the route. *Officers* kept the crew at their jobs. Sometimes the officers had their own servants.

*Seamen* heaved on ropes to move the sails into the right place to catch the wind. The ship was steered by a rudder at the back. One seaman moved the tiller, the handle of the rudder, to make the ship turn right or left.

*Carpenters* shaped planks to replace leaky ones. They made new masts if any were damaged in a storm.

*Cooks* prepared food for all the crew. They had to be very careful not to set the wooden ship on fire.

*Cabin boys* helped with all these jobs and fed the animals being carried for food.

*The ship's doctor* kept medicine in pots and gave injections with a syringe. He used a wooden mallet and a knife to amputate limbs.

**Ship's carpenter**

**Ship's doctor**

**Main hatch**

**Store of sails, ropes and other equipment.**

**The stone ballast helped to make the ship stable.**

**This is what Magellan's ship *Trinidad* may have looked like inside.**

▲ These things were taken on board a ship called the *Mary Rose* in the 15th century.

Main cabin – for officers and gentlemen.

The steersman pulled the tiller which moved the big rudder and directed the ship.

Sail maker

Stores of food and water.

## Scurvy

Many sailors who went on long voyages became ill or even died from a disease called scurvy. Their legs and gums swelled. They were covered with spots and were too tired to move. One man wrote, "The gums of our men grew so much that they could not eat, and nineteen died." They did not know that scurvy was caused by not eating fresh fruit and vegetables.

# Finding the way

When ships sail out of sight of land the captain has to work out which direction to steer the ship in. This is called navigation. Modern ships have many special instruments which tell the captain exactly where he is. But in the 'Age of Exploration' navigation was much more difficult. Explorers had to work out where north, south, east and west were. They also had to work out how fast the ship was moving and how long they had been at sea.

▲ **An astrolabe.**

◄ **An hour-glass.** Sailors warmed the glass so that the sand would run through more quickly. This affected the navigation, so bars were added to make warming the glass difficult.

## Finding the equator ▶

At midday the captain used an astrolabe or quadrant to measure how far the sun was above his head. He then looked at charts and lists that helped him work out how far north or south of the <u>equator</u> he was.

## ◄ Finding north

The captain used a compass to find out in which direction he was heading. The iron needle always pointed towards the north.

He could also study the stars at night. The group of stars called the Plough helped him find the <u>Pole Star</u>, which was in the north.

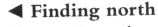

## Finding east and west ▶

It was much more difficult to find out how far east or west he had sailed from his home port. To work this out he needed to know how long he had been travelling. For this a really reliable clock was needed. Explorers used an hour-glass filled with sand. A cabin boy had to keep turning the hour-glass and counting the hours. Telling the time this way was not very accurate.

## ◀ Finding the speed of the ship

The captain could only guess how far his ship had sailed every day. To do this he had to work out how fast the ship was travelling, allowing for currents. He used a 'log', a bit of wood on the end of a line with knots a certain distance apart. The line was thrown into the sea and the knots were counted to show how far the ship had sailed from the wood in a certain time. Today a ship's speed is still counted in 'knots'.

# Christopher Columbus

Christopher Columbus was born in Genoa in Italy in 1451. He was the son of a poor weaver and so did not go to school. But Columbus taught himself to read and write and he studied books about explorers and navigation. He went to work as a sailor when he was very young and soon decided to make a voyage of exploration himself.

Columbus was sure that he could find a way to China by sailing west from Spain. To do this he would have to sail across the Atlantic Ocean, with no maps to guide him.

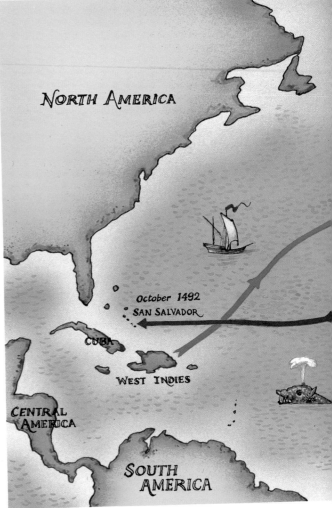

He had to find someone to pay for the voyage. The King of Portugal refused, so Columbus went to the King and Queen of Spain. It was six years before they agreed to help him.

▲ Christopher Columbus.

We Vikings travelled to America hundreds of years before Columbus.

ATLANTIC OCEAN

Lisbon

PORTUGAL

Palos

August 1492

CANARY ISLANDS
September 1492

AFRICA

VOYAGE of COLUMBUS

We were all living in America long before the Vikings arrived.

## The voyage of Columbus

In 1492, Columbus set sail with three ships to the Canary Islands, then west into unknown waters. After a month, the sailors were very discontented. Some men wanted to throw Columbus overboard and go home.

But at last they arrived at an island in the Bahamas. Columbus thought he was near the coast of China, but he did not realize that China was very much further away.

Friendly Indians took Columbus to other islands. He thought the big island of Cuba was China, where there was said to be a lot of gold. He was disappointed that the Indians did not have very much gold, but he traded red sailors' caps and necklaces of glass beads for lumps of gold.

Columbus returned home with some Indians, parrots, and other things that the people of Spain were amazed to see. Columbus was famous at last!

## The great discovery

Columbus made some mistakes. He was sure he had reached China. But he had in fact almost reached the continent we now call North and South America. If he had sailed only a little further, he would have found all the gold of the great empires of the Aztecs and the Incas. However, his maps and stories made other explorers want to follow him into the unknown, to what was called the 'New World'.

# Maps of the world

If you were going to travel around the world today you could take an atlas with you. The maps in the atlas show exactly what all the countries of the world look like. We know our maps are correct because we have taken photographs of the earth from space.

In 1450 no one knew exactly what the earth looked like. Explorers had to use maps that had been drawn by other explorers and sailors. These maps were not very accurate. But by the end of the 'Age of Exploration', Europeans had a much better idea of what the world looked like.

▶ Map of the world as known in 1570. You can see how much of the world had been mapped by explorers during the 'Age of Exploration'. The words at the bottom of the map say 'the unknown land to the south'.

▼ Map of the world made in the AD 100s by an Ancient Greek geographer called Claudius Ptolemy. You can see that the huge continent of America is missing. This map was still being used by explorers in 1490.

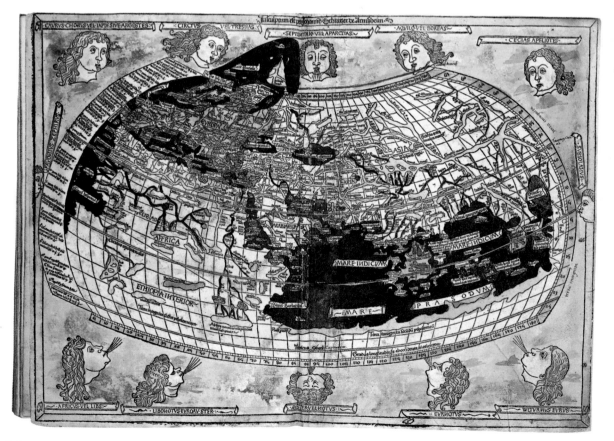

16

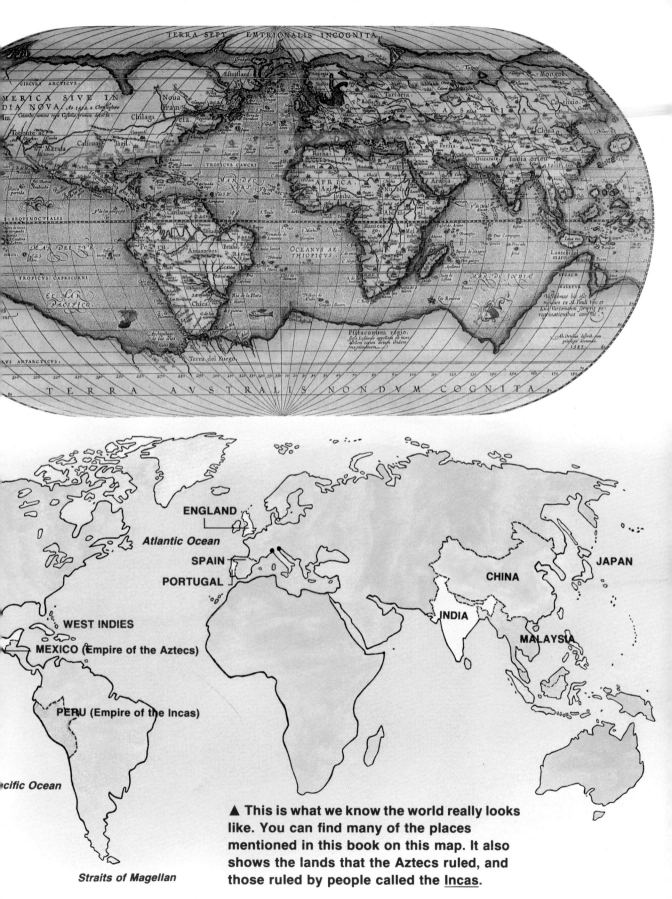

▲ This is what we know the world really looks like. You can find many of the places mentioned in this book on this map. It also shows the lands that the Aztecs ruled, and those ruled by people called the <u>Incas</u>.

# EMPIRE OF THE AZTECS

The Spanish explorers who followed Columbus found a land of high mountains, dusty deserts, swamps and steamy jungles. This was the land we now call Mexico. Many different tribes of people lived there. The strongest tribe of them all was called the Aztecs.

The Aztecs were fierce warriors. They had conquered many other tribes and had built a huge empire. When another tribe had been defeated in battle they had to send gifts to the Aztec emperor. As long as they sent these gifts they were allowed to live as they wanted and worship their own gods.

**Aztecs paying <u>tribute</u> to their emperor, Montezuma.**

## Aztec law

The Aztecs had strict laws which everyone had to obey. Judges heard cases in the Law Courts. People could be put to death for wearing sandals when they visited the emperor or for stealing. Some thieves had to work as slaves until they had paid back twice the value of what was stolen. If one man attacked another, he had to pay for making the victim well and for any damage.

If an Aztec man lied in court he was put to death. However, we Aztecs did not torture people to make them tell the truth like the Spaniards did.

People who stole crops were killed, but the law made sure that maize, beans and squashes were planted along roads for poor people to take.

Nobles and officials were punished more severely than common people, as they were expected to set an example of good behaviour.

# Aztec people

The Aztecs were ruled over by an emperor who lived in a palace in the chief city, Tenochtitlan. Other important people were the nobles who worked as judges, priests, officials or merchants.

Most people were farmers or craftsmen. They belonged to family clans. Each clan lived in one part of a city led by a head man. The head man divided up clan land for the farmers to grow food.

Nearly all Aztec men, whether they were important officials or just farmers, also had to be soldiers. No man could become a noble unless he had fought in battle and captured four enemies.

**◄ Priests**
The Aztecs believed their priests could foretell the future. Priests worshipped the gods and sacrificed prisoners taken in battle. Priests and priestesses also taught the children of nobles how to read and write. Priests were not allowed to cut or wash their hair, or to marry.

**► Farmers**
Farmers worked on the land, growing maize which was ground into flour.

**► Slaves**
Slaves were usually prisoners captured during battles with other tribes. Hardworking slaves could earn goods to buy their freedom.

## ▼ Merchants

Merchants were often rich but they were not allowed to show off by wearing fine clothes and jewellery. Merchants often went on long expeditions to trade. They carried news about and brought information to the emperor.

## ▲ Soldiers

Aztec soldiers wore costumes of padded cotton. Their shields were decorated with feathers or paint. The best soldiers became eagle or jaguar knights and wore special costumes.

Boys were sent to school to learn how to fight. They practised with wooden shields and clubs.

## Clothes

Clothes were very important to the Aztecs. They were like a uniform. They showed who a person was. Chiefs wore special headbands. Soldiers wore bright cloaks and feather head-dresses. Poor men wore a loincloth and a cloak knotted on one shoulder. Women wore skirts with a belt and a sleeveless shirt. People could be put to death for wearing clothes that made them look more important than they were.

# Island city

The greatest city of the Aztecs was called Tenochtitlan. (Tenochtitlan means "place of the prickly pear cactus".) It was built on a swampy island which was in the middle of a lake. The Aztecs felt safe from their enemies on the island.

**Chinampas**

**Three main causeways linked the city to the mainland.**

**The great square**

**The city of Tenochtitlan, built on an island in the middle of Lake Texcoco.**

It was difficult to grow crops on the swampy ground, so the Aztecs made small square gardens in the shallow water round the island. These gardens were called chinampas. (You can find out more about chinampas on page 30.) As more chinampas were made, the island grew bigger, and people built houses and temples on the new land.

There were earth pathways in the city, but most people travelled about in canoes. The island was joined to the shore by three causeways. These had moveable bridges to let canoes pass through. Fresh water was brought from the shore in an <u>aqueduct</u> of clay pipes.

Most houses in Tenochtitlan had a kind of sauna, people also bathed in the lake. All over the city were canoes used as public lavatories. These were emptied onto the chinampas to make the crops grow.

**People travelled about the city in canoes.**

**The main temple dominated the city. It was over 50 metres tall, and decorated with stone carvings.**

**Skull rack**

## The great square

In the centre of the city was a great square, where the temples of the gods stood on high platforms. They towered above the houses and the emperor's palaces. Tenochtitlan was bigger than any city in Europe at that time. But it must have been a smelly place, especially in the central square. Thousands of heads of sacrificed victims lay rotting on a great skull rack. The long temple staircases were dark with blood from human sacrifices.

23

# Aztec technology

## Tools

The Aztecs built large cities and made many beautiful things using very simple tools. They did not know how to make things from iron, like weapons or spades. They used wooden sticks to dig their fields.

The Aztecs made many tools and objects from obsidian, a black, glassy rock formed from volcanic lava. The Aztecs chipped obsidian to make very sharp knives. Obsidian was also polished with sand to make mirrors, ornaments and masks.

▲ An Aztec mask made from polished obsidian.

◄ Stone hammers were used to shape stone into statues of gods and goddesses. This is a carving of an Aztec goddess.

24

Important people travelled in a litter carried on men's shoulders.

A bride was carried to her wedding on the back of an older woman who had helped to arrange the marriage.

Merchants transported their goods in canoes hollowed out by fire.

## Weapons

Aztec soldiers did not have metal swords like the Spaniards. They made axe heads out of copper, but copper is not hard enough to make a sword. Aztec soldiers used swords made from wood, about one metre long. Along each edge of the sword was a groove fitted with obsidian blades. These swords were very sharp, but they soon became blunt or broken in battle. They also used arrows tipped with obsidian.

## Transport

The Aztecs did not have horses or oxen to pull carts and heavy loads. On land, porters carried heavy loads. They tied headbands around their foreheads to help take the weight of the load. Large blocks of stone were moved by rolling them along on logs.

The Aztecs did not use the wheel. Aztec children played with toys that had little wheels, but Aztec roads were too rough for larger wheeled carts.

# Aztec houses

The Aztecs used wood, stone and adobe to build their houses and palaces. Adobe bricks were made of clay and chopped straw, dried in the sun.

## A poor family's home
Ordinary people lived in wooden huts with a thatched roof of reeds. There was only one room.

▲ The bottom of this Aztec bowl is very rough. It may have been used to grind peppercorns.

Aztec huts were made from wood, stone and adobe. The roof was thatched with reeds.

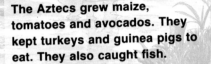

The Aztecs grew maize, tomatoes and avocados. They kept turkeys and guinea pigs to eat. They also caught fish.

There was an open fire in the hut. The Aztecs cooked flat corn pancakes called <u>tortillas</u> on a clay <u>griddle</u> that rested over the fire.

Aztec houses had stone foundations and were built of brick. Wooden pillars held up the beam over the doorways.

Curtains were used to separate the rooms.

The Aztecs did not have much furniture. They kept clothes in chests of wood or basketwork.

In the middle of the courtyard was a fountain and pool of water.

Some rooms had a fireplace. Fires were lit by twirling a hard stick on a soft board.

Beds were reed mats on the floor.

The Aztecs lit fires in clay bowls with legs. The fire provided heat and light, and could be moved from room to room.

## A rich family's home

Houses of rich families had many rooms. Some stood on a platform between two and twelve metres high. The outer walls were covered with plaster and painted white or dark red. Rooms were built around a courtyard cooled by a fountain. A string of bells, which rang when people entered or left the house, hung across the doorway.

# Religion and sacrifice

The Aztecs were very religious. They worshipped many gods and goddesses. They made statues of their gods and placed them in their temples. Some Aztec priests believed that all the gods were part of a single god or creator called the 'Lord of Everywhere'. But they did not make statues of this god.

All Aztecs were brought up to tell the truth and be good citizens, but they believed that where you went after death depended on how you died. People who were sacrificed to the gods went to heaven. Those who died of old age went to an underworld.

## Human sacrifices to the gods

The Aztecs believed that sacrificing people would keep the gods happy and prevent disasters. Many gods and goddesses were believed to control the weather. People made sacrifices to them to make crops grow, to keep storms away, and to send rain at the right time.

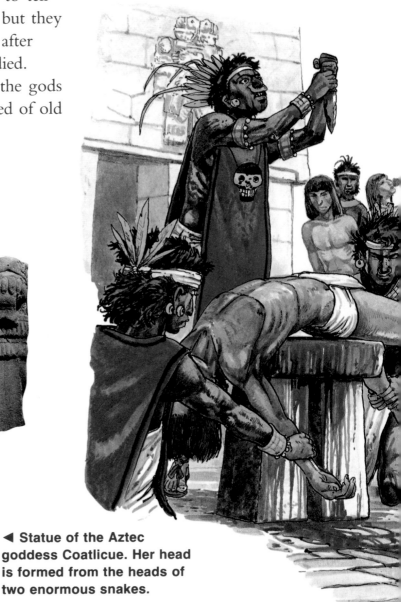

◀ Statue of the Aztec goddess Coatlicue. Her head is formed from the heads of two enormous snakes.

Children were sacrificed to the god Tlaloc, which means 'he who makes things grow'. The Aztecs believed that the tears of children would make the rain fall on their crops. So the more the children were made to cry, the more rain would fall.

The Aztecs believed in a sun god called Huitzilopochtli. They believed that every night he had to fight against the forces of darkness so that the sun would rise in the morning. To help him do this they cut out the hearts of prisoners captured in war, which they offered as food to the sun god.

Captives were sacrificed by priests at the top of temples. One by one the captives climbed the temple steps. They were held over a stone and the priest cut out their hearts with a sharp knife.

The body was then hurled down the temple steps and cut up. Parts were eaten by priests and by the warrior who had captured the man. The rest was fed to the animals in the emperor's zoo. The head was put on the skull rack.

▲ Aztec carving of a skull rack. Skull racks were used to store the heads of sacrificed enemy warriors. Every Aztec temple had a skull rack nearby.

## The New Fire Festival

There were many religious festivals during the year. People danced in bright costumes, and sang chants. Boys and girls learned these chants at music schools.

Every 52 years the Aztecs feared that the world would come to an end. To stop this happening they held the 'New Fire Festival'. All fires were put out until certain stars appeared that told the priests that the world was safe again. Everyone then lit new fires, put on new clothes, and held feasts to celebrate.

29

# Food and farming

There were no cows, sheep or pigs in Mexico until they were brought by the Spaniards. For meat, the Aztecs ate deer and small fattened hairless dogs. They ate fish from the lakes and rivers. Rich people ate crabs, oysters and sea fish, brought 200 miles from the coast to inland cities by special runners. Rich people also ate many other kinds of special dishes.

Many vegetables were grown such as tomatoes, peppers and avocado pears. These grew especially well in the damp ground of the chinampas.

The Aztecs' main food was <u>maize</u>. Women spent many hours each day preparing it. Maize flour was made into <u>tortillas</u>, which were like pancakes. These were eaten with spicy sauces. Maize porridge was sweetened with honey or plant syrup.

In a good year, a family grew more maize than they needed, and could take it to the market to trade. But if the crops died from frost or lack of rain the family would starve. No wonder they prayed to the gods of weather!

## Chinampas

Farmers at Tenochtitlan made chinampas to grow their vegetables. First they wove fences and fixed them around a square of shallow water with posts. Then they filled the squares with water plants and mud from the lake. These chinampas could be as big as 200 metres square. Vegetables are still grown this way in Mexico today.

> We loved tortillas stuffed with frogs, snails and tadpoles.

▶ **Every city had a market, with strict rules and special police. People did not buy with coins, but exchanged goods. Cocoa beans were used as a kind of money.**

Wooden sticks were used to dig the soil.

Fences were woven and built around each chinampa to keep the water out.

The chinampas were filled with plants, dirt and mud to make the swampy ground suitable for growing crops.

Aztec chinampas.

# Clothes and crafts

Aztec craftspeople made many beautiful objects out of obsidian, gold, jade and turquoise. They also made fine painted pottery bowls, figures and flutes. Many of these objects were lost, stolen or destroyed after the Spanish conquest.

▲ Jewellery was a sign of importance to the Aztecs. This is an Aztec ear-ring.

▼ What feathers were used to make the animal design on this Aztec warrior's shield?

▲ Aztec women wove cloth on looms that were held around the waist.

◄ Mosaic-workers stuck tiny bits of turquoise onto wood to make wonderful masks. This is a mosaic mask of the god Quetzalcoatl.

## Weaving cloth

Aztec women wove cloth that was coloured yellow, blue, violet, green and black, with plant dyes. Red dye was made from squashed cochineal beetles which lived on cactus plants at special Aztec farms.

Girls were taught to spin and weave by their mothers. They wove cloth on a type of loom that is still used in Mexico today.

Clothes were sewn with needles made from the cactus spines. These were also stuck into lazy children!

## Feather-workers

Feather-workers were a special group of craftspeople. They made special ornaments and the costumes worn by priests and warriors. The feathers were brought as <u>tribute</u> by other tribes. The feather-workers used the brilliant green feathers of the quetzal bird, the red of the roseate spoonbill, the yellow of parrots and the turquoise of humming birds.

The women sorted the feathers and the men stuck them in place with glue which the children made from bat dung.

# Writing and counting

Most Aztecs were farmers and did not learn to read and write. Only children who were going to grow up to be nobles or priests were taught to read and write.

Officials had to write lists of goods sent to the emperor as <u>tribute</u>. Scribes wrote down what was said in the Law Courts. Maps were made showing who owned each bit of land in case of arguments. Priests wrote down ancient legends and the history of their tribe. They also wrote about stars and planets.

▲ Aztec books were called codex. This codex is made of deerskin pages which are painted on both sides.

▼ This picture from an Aztec book shows the Aztec god Tezcatlipoca tempting the Earth Monster to come to the surface of the sea. He is using his foot as bait.

## Aztec books

Aztec books were different from ours. They were not printed, but written by hand on both sides of a long strip of paper, deerskin, or cloth made from a cactus. Paper was made from the inner bark of a fig tree, which was soaked and hammered with a stone beater. The strip was folded and wooden covers were glued to the ends.

## Signs for words and numbers

Aztec books were not written in words, but in pictures or signs. Some pictures stood for sounds. Other signs stood for numbers. The Aztecs counted in 20s. What do you think gave them this idea?

**These are Aztec signs for numbers.**

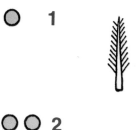

O 1

OO 2

400

20

8,000

40

**These are Aztec signs for words.**

**This is the sign for a rabbit.**

**This is the sign for an alligator.**

**This sign means movement.**

**The sign for Tepetitlan, an Aztec city, was made from two other signs.**

**A mountain (tepetl)**

**with teeth (tlanti)**

**Tepetitlan.**

35

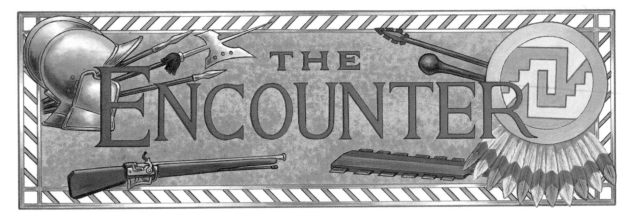

# THE ENCOUNTER

## Montezuma the emperor

When an Aztec emperor died, the council of priests and nobles chose one of the men in his family to be the next ruler. Montezuma was only 22 years old when he was crowned emperor of the Aztecs in 1520. He was chosen because he was a wise priest and a brave soldier.

Montezuma lived in a palace in Tenochtitlan. Only the most important officials were allowed to go to the palace to hear his orders. Montezuma was emperor and chief priest, but a council of priests and nobles did the work of ruling the empire. People only saw the emperor during ceremonies.

He was served by beautiful girls, and washed his hands between courses. He did not eat or drink very much, although every day 300 dishes were cooked for him to choose from. He was offered stewed duck, frogs with chillies, venison with chillies and tomatoes, locusts with sage, quail and turkey.

After the evening meal, he drank chocolate; crushed cocoa beans boiled with maize flour and whisked into a froth. He smoked tobacco in a silver tube before going to sleep.

◄ This is what a Spaniard wrote about Montezuma's meals.

## The legend of Quetzalcoatl

Montezuma knew all about Aztec history and legends and believed that movements of the stars and planets affected life on earth.

Montezuma knew of one important Aztec legend that said that the god Quetzalcoatl would one day come to the land of the Aztecs. This dark-haired god had a black beard, which was unusual among Aztecs. Legend said that this god would appear in the Aztec year One Reed, which means 1519.

▶ Hernando Cortes.

▲ This Aztec sculpture shows the head of the Aztec god Quetzalcoatl coming out of the jaws of the Earth Monster.

## The Spaniards arrive

After Columbus returned to Spain and told people about the West Indies, young men sailed out there to make their fortunes.

One of these men was Hernando Cortes. He was a brave soldier and liked adventure. He had heard the stories of explorers who had reached the coast of Mexico. They told of marvellous stone buildings and gold objects.

The Spanish governor of Cuba agreed to send Cortes, with 600 men, to seize Mexico for the King of Spain.

# Cortes the conqueror

At the first place where Cortes landed, he was attacked by an army of 12,000 Indians. But Cortes and his men had swords, muskets, cannons and horses. They defeated the Indians and killed many who were unarmed.

The defeated Indians gave Cortes valuable gifts, and an Indian girl called Malinche. Cortes called her Marina.

Marina learned to speak Spanish. She loved Cortes, and helped him to plan his conquest of Mexico.

Cortes decided to attack the powerful Aztecs. Many of the Indians Cortes had captured agreed to help him. They hated the Aztecs because they had to give a lot of their crops as tribute to Montezuma every year.

**The Indians of Central America had never seen guns, armour or horses before. Some thought that the men on horses were one strange animal.**

▲ This double-headed serpent may have been one of the gifts Montezuma sent to Cortes. It was worn around the neck by a high priest.

## Gifts for a god

Messengers arrived in Tenochtitlan with news of these strange bearded people with pale faces and strange clothes. Montezuma thought that their leader must be the god Quetzalcoatl.

Cortes sailed along the coast to meet Montezuma's messengers. He landed on Friday 22nd April 1519, which was the very year and day that legend said that Quetzalcoatl would return!

Montezuma sent gifts of beautiful things. He hoped these gifts would make the god happy and go back home. But they only made Cortes determined to stay and seize this land of gold for the Spanish King.

## On to Tenochtitlan

Cortes decided to march to the great Aztec city, Tenochtitlan. He was worried that many of his men would refuse to follow him, so he sank all his ships. There was no going back!

The journey to Tenochtitlan was terrible. They had to cross hot, steamy swamps full of mosquitoes, and mountains with icy winds. Many of Cortes's men died on the journey.

# The fall of Tenochtitlan

When Cortes arrived in Tenochtitlan he was amazed at the size of the city. He called Tenochtitlan 'the most beautiful city in the world'.

Cortes met Montezuma face to face and was invited to live in a palace next to the great temple in Tenochtitlan. But the Spaniards soon became unhappy. Every day they saw men sacrificed to the sun god. They were horrified by the Aztecs' skull rack.

> The Spaniards thought we were cruel, but they killed and tortured many people.

Cortes didn't trust Montezuma, so he took him hostage. Cortes then returned to the coast leaving some of his men in charge. On the next festival day the dancing Aztecs filled the main square. Cortes's men panicked and began shooting the Aztecs. In the fighting that followed Montezuma himself was killed. Many Spaniards also died as they fled the city.

## The attack

Cortes spent nearly a year preparing to capture Tenochtitlan, with help from many Indian tribes. He stopped canoes taking food across the lake to the city and many Aztecs starved. Cortes attacked with horses and cannons. The Aztecs were massacred and the whole city destroyed. Cortes was now the ruler of Mexico, Spain's new empire.

▲ This picture was painted in the early 18th century. It shows Cortes and the Spanish army crossing the causeway to the Aztec island city, Tenochtitlan.

# The end of the Aztecs

### Waging war

The entire Aztec empire had been conquered by only a few hundred Spaniards. One of the reasons why the Spaniards were so successful was because the Aztecs did not understand the Spanish way of fighting. Aztec soldiers went into battle to try to capture their enemies. They wanted to take live captives home to sacrifice. They did not expect to be killed in battle.

They hungered like pigs for that gold.

▼ **This 18th century painting shows the Spanish army at Tenochtitlan's city gates.**

## Religion

When the Aztecs defeated another tribe they allowed that tribe to carry on worshipping their own gods. But the rulers of Spain, from the time of Columbus, wanted the people of all lands to be told about the Christian God. After the fall of Tenochtitlan, Christian <u>friars</u> went to Mexico. They <u>baptised</u> many Indians and tried to stop all worship of the Aztec gods. Aztec men were made to cover their legs with trousers.

▶ **The Spaniards destroyed the Aztec temples and statues. They believed that this would make the Aztecs forget their gods and become Christians.**

Aztec temples were pulled down. The stones were used to build Christian churches. Many Aztec books were burnt. Beautiful golden Aztec objects were melted down. The gold was sent back to Spain.

## Disease

The Spaniards killed many Aztecs with their guns, cannons and horsemen. But they killed many more with diseases that they brought with them. Aztecs died from diseases that only made Europeans ill, like measles and influenza. Thousands died of smallpox, tuberculosis, malaria and yellow fever.

# Spain's new empire

After the conquest, Mexico was called 'New Spain'. Expeditions were sent from Mexico to explore North and South America. A Spaniard called Pizarro conquered the Incas of Peru. He made them work in silver mines. A lot of silver was sent to Spain, but many Indians died in the mines.

In the West Indies, Spaniards grew sugar cane in plantations. But so many of their Indian workers died that black slaves were brought from West Africa as labourers. Their descendants still live in the West Indies.

## The Spanish impact

The Spaniards brought their own technology to the 'New World'. They used wheeled vehicles, the plough, and iron tools. They used their alphabet for writing, and coins for buying goods instead of bartering. They introduced animals from Europe to eat, like cattle, sheep, pigs and goats. Horses were also introduced to carry people and loads, and to pull wagons.

New towns with Spanish names were built. The buildings in them were made in the Spanish style.

**Spanish explorers brought back many new foods from the empire of the Aztecs.**

## The Mexican forests

The Aztecs used a lot of wood in their kilns. They also used wood to make their homes and canoes. But the Aztecs were careful to preserve their forests. People were killed if they cut down a tree for firewood, but they could collect dead wood.

The Spaniards used more wood than the Aztecs. They also cleared forests to make farms. The animals they bred ate the shoots of young trees, so that new trees could not grow. Now the great forests of Ancient Mexico have gone.

## New things to eat

The Aztecs and other tribes in the 'New World' grew food plants that were not known then in Europe. Plants like maize were taken home by the Spanish conquerors. Other foods brought back included cocoa beans, pumpkins, peppers and pineapples. Farmers in Europe were able to grow far more food on their land than ever before.

Besides the useful things from the 'New World' came the harmful plant, tobacco. It was smoked by the Indians in tubes. People in Europe were amazed to see men smoking.

Sir Walter Raleigh was an Englishman who went to the 'New World' near the end of the 16th century. There is a story that one of his servants saw him smoking and thought his master was on fire. The servant threw a bucket of water over him.

# What happened to the Aztecs?

The Spaniards destroyed the Aztec empire, their laws, and the way the people were ruled by their councils and emperor. The people had to obey Spanish law and become Christians.

Life in Mexico today is a mixture of Spanish and Indian ways. Mexicans celebrate the great Christian festivals with singing and dancing in colourful costumes—just as their Aztec ancestors had celebrated the festivals of their old gods and goddesses. In some towns men dress as jaguars and fight with whips. They say they do it to bring rain. Children dress up too.

Some Aztec food is still eaten. People make tortillas, you will find these being made in Spain too. Mexican people still weave colourful cloth on looms like those the Aztecs used. The Aztec language is still spoken in many parts of Mexico.

Most of the beautiful things made by the Aztecs and other Indian craftsmen were destroyed. Luckily, a few still remain to remind us of the skill of the Aztec craftspeople.

▲ This human skull is now in the Museum of Mankind in London. It is covered with blue turquoise and other precious stones. It has leather straps to tie it round a warrior's waist.

▲ One of the few Aztec temples that remain in Mexico today.

Remains of Aztec temples can also be seen in Mexico today. They remind us of the great civilisation of the Aztecs. It is amazing to think that these temples were built by people who did not have any machines to help them. They did not even use metal tools or the wheel.

▶ Aztec stone carving.

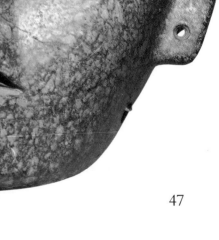

# Glossary

These words are <u>underlined</u> in this book.

**Ancestors**
People from whom you are descended.

**Aqueduct**
A channel or pipe carrying water from its source to where it is needed.

**Baptised**
When someone becomes a Christian they are sprinkled with water, or baptised, to welcome them into the Christian church.

**Currents**
Streams of flowing water in the oceans that affect the speed and the direction of ships.

**Equator**
An imaginary line drawn around the earth dividing north from south.

**Friars**
Christian monks who worked among people instead of living in a monastery.

**Griddle**
A flat clay slab that is placed over a fire and used for baking on.

**Incas**
American people who established an empire in the mountains of Peru in South America.

**Maize**
A cereal plant similar to sweetcorn. The Aztecs ground it to make flour.

**Maya**
American people who established an empire in Central America.

**Pole Star**
The Pole Star is in the group of stars that we call the Plough or Dipper. It shows the direction of north, and so helped explorers to find their way.

**Satellite**
A spacecraft that circles the earth and sends pictures and other information back to Earth.

**Silk**
A material woven from the threads produced by a silk worm when it makes its cocoon.

**Tortillas**
Round, flat cakes made of maize flour, cooked on a griddle and eaten with a savoury filling.

**Tribute**
Payment of food or other things from a conquered tribe to the conqueror.